A Reckless Descent from Eternity

For Deb Westbury

Anne Morgan

A Reckless Descent from Eternity

The Poems

Many poems in *A Reckless Descent from Eternity* have won or have been placed or commended in literary competitions including *Island*'s Gwen Harwood Poetry Award, *Overland*'s Judith Wright Poetry Award, the Orange Arts Council's Banjo Paterson Award and several Fellowship of Australian Writers Tasmania (FAWTAS) awards. Earlier versions of poems published here have appeared in the journals *Island*, *New England Review*, *Blue Giraffe*, *The Mozzie*, *Thirst*, *Famous Reporter*, *Marginata*, *RePUBlic Readings*, *The Poets' Republic*, and in the *Weekend Australian Review*. Some poems have been re-published in the anthologies *Running through the Stars*, FAWTAS, 2004, *A River of Verse*, Black River Press, 2004, *Mood Cumulus*, Central Coast Writers, 2005, *The Weighing of the Heart*, Sunline Press, 2007, *A Net of Hands*, FAWTAS 2009, and in the chapbook *Echoes from the Firetrails*, Tom Collins House, 2004. Certain poems in this collection have also been published online in *The Write Stuff Showcase of Tasmanian Poetry and Tasmanian Times*.

Acknowledgements

I am grateful to the Varuna Writers Centre for sponsoring a mentorship to work on the completion of this manuscript. Heartfelt thanks to my poetry mentor, Deb Westbury, for her boundless insight and encouragement. Thanks also to John Warren for editorial assistance and generous bootloads of firewood and organic vegetables. I would also like to acknowledge the vibrant and talented writing communities of Tasmania and Western Australia, particularly Anne Kellas and Helen Brett, and my mother, Claire Morgan, for unstinting support. Thanks also to the 'Cascades Dawn Mafia' for walks and talks on the mountain. Finally, thanks to Stephen Matthews of Ginninderra Press, for accepting and publishing this manuscript, and for being such a stalwart champion of emerging Australian writers.

A Reckless Descent from Eternity
ISBN 978 1 74027 579 8
Copyright © text Anne Morgan 2009
Cover image: *Chimneys*, by Adrian Donoghue

First published 2009
Reprinted 2016

GINNINDERRA PRESS
PO Box 3461 Port Adelaide SA 5015
www.ginninderrapress.com.au

Contents

Solstice Night Walk	7
Reflection	8
Echoes From the Fire Trails	9
Mountain Ruins	10
Winterspring	11
Flying On	12
Angel Mist	13
Currawongs	14
Hermitage	15
Thunderdown Gondwana	16
Inglewood Road, Cascades	17
Antipodean May Day	18
Fishing For Stars, Tiananmen Square, 2001	19
Aeroplane Awakening	22
Old Farm Road	23
Weedy Sea Dance	24
Iceberg	25
Bass Strait Sealers	26
An Unknown Wreck, Macquarie Island	27
Bellerive's Old Fort	29
Buckley Under the Playground	31
Spiritlands Undreaming	33
Fifteenth Summer	37
Seventeenth Winter	38
Valuing	39
Secateurs	40
The Beginning of Wonders, Marakoopa	41
Through Paradise, Running On Empty	44
Devil's Lookout	45
Small Expectations	46

Seeking the Alpha Male	47
Domestos	48
Interview	49
Sphinx Rock	50
Great Oyster Bay Before a Storm	51
Pilgrimage, 1980	53
The Calliag	54
The Gap	56
Mickey Fadgy's Ulster	57
Busking Angel, Perth	59
Rules For Living In a Postbox	60
National Poetry Week	61
Wildflower Show, King's Park	62
Bread Upon the Waters, Lake Jualbup	63
Statue of the Arts, Albany	65
Villanelle For Miranda	66
Inheritance	67
Butterfly Road	68
Learning To Love Fragments	70
The Sweetening Shadows	73

Solstice Night Walk

Orion ascends a rooftop constellation
of elf and sleigh and reindeer
as I tread the leafy edges
of the shortest dark,
wind-chimed in jasmine.

My dog is travelling on a baser plane,
tracking urine scents on scribbled bark
and poles of swamp or blue gum,
stripped and wired and copper-chromed.

A screech of brushtail claws
the blackboard of the night.
Fear pumps blood through smaller hearts.
A furry shadow shoots the bitumen
and vanishes in a brake shriek.

Reflection

No snapping switch brings instant light to the farmhouse.
I light five candles while my children bluster,
then stoke the range for the evening's cooking.
Outside the window, an apple tree probes in the sunset
the secrets of centuries buried in the unpruned orchard.

This tree once flourished like the farmhouse families
in sun, mist and silence truncated
by guns and chainsaws, bellows and bleats,
the echoing hoots of amorous owls
and the fractured echoes of laughter,
yet still its lichen-scabbed trunk sluices sap
to its branches, seasoned with snow or blossom,
and, summer-leaf green,
raucous with parrots and wattlebirds,
or gravid with apples and children.
And still it scrabbles, swollen-jointed,
to survive my grandchildren's grandchildren.

I see the vision sideways and turn to stare again:
framed in red cedar, reflected through glass,
the budding ghosts of five candles burn merrily
as Christmas, Beltane or Lughnasa
in the branches of its withering.

Echoes From the Fire Trails

When the fire trails were radiant
with wattle blossom, I ran the slopes
of the mountain, steadying my heartbeat
at Ki Creek, where the council had fenced
and planted a sign, warning the wary
that the water was deep.

I searched for a platypus in cool, liquid shadows,
sloughing off years spent indoors,
when fluorescent lights flicked and flashed,
and the air was still and dry.
Storm clouds packed, tightly as a choir
preparing to rehearse a Passion
as the mountain cockatoos squalled,
bringing wind-washed hopes to my mind
which were welcome as a platypus
or endorphins in tears.

Mountain Ruins

I found them one lost autumn
when wattles were tipping purple
by tackling the switchback track
where sassafras and dogwood
stood sentinel to a gallery of fungi –
a low stone rectangle,
chimney footings within;
beyond, a moss-rugged mound
where claret parasols and orange crinolines
turned petticoat-high to the leering sun.
Yellow hands of sponge coral
shrank away to a liverwort gloom
where staghorns reared
by the chattering falls
of a time-slipped stream.

Winterspring

A horse clops down the winding seconds.
Chills creep through the interstices
of night and light and cramp along my femurs.
I seal the draught between skin and featherdown
until the first and final bus
of Sunday morning rumbles by.

Begrudging the quotidian,
I slink out, book in hand, to the fire trails,
to follow wraiths of sunlight along the melting foothills,
leaving body-prints in grass
to the manic energies of grasshoppers
and the pert gyrations of pretty-boy wrens,
until, bounding through bracken and fishback fern,
my dog invades my story with a passionate devotion,
and the heroine knows true love at last.

Flying On

Those innocent eyes
could not melt to mawkishness
the butcher beak that stabbed
between two mornings.

I could have shielded that young kookaburra,
cradled him in polartech,
put him to roost with the chooks in my lemon tree,
although his beak would have grown
cruel enough to prey on tiger snakes
and to laugh rudely outside my window.
Instead, I left him fledging on a charred log
where a sprig of mountain pepper
burst like an artery.

Next morning, when we surveyed a bloodied mess
of feathers on dry leaf humus,
you declared it was no longer him.
And I recalled another bushfire sunrise
on the Middle Island track,
when you described the murdered bodies of your sister
and nine-year-old niece.
You said they had flown on.
I envied then your ingenuous eyes,
your freedom to fly on.

Angel Mist

Before the aurora shocked your optic nerve
and vaporised your orange sunset,
before you bathed in angel mist
and handed down covenants
that would save the world from evol
which is love spelled backwards,
we followed torchlight moons on frosted branches,
watched glow worms in their pearl-blue snarings
and from Sphinx Rock
looked down on this river-bound
and light-reflected city.

You dispensed wisdom
decaffeinated from your teapot
and were an oracle
before your epiphany.
Today you're just yourself,
but much more so,
though now you choose
to be a lunatic
because, you say,
they kill the prophets,
don't they?

Currawongs

A rooster cries falsetto
above the basso profundo
of my neighbour's ewe
as I lie in a hollow of longed-for sleep
after the violation of last night's storm.

Outside my window
the veranda rail shudders.
I draw curtains to a gold-ringed gaze
that vanishes in a head swish.

A currawong wears his blindness
like a corsair's eye patch.
Brandishing his rapier beak,
he broadcasts his call to action

and a murder of currawongs replies,
raining on branches of lemon and judas trees
while their one-eyed leader stands defiant,
daring me to reclaim my jacket
which lies like a corpse beneath claws,
frost-stung on the veranda.

Hermitage

He greets snakes and frogmouths into visibility,
musters scarlet robins with hand-held cheese,
asks after their families,
and they don't seem to mind
his incessant chipperings.

His fountain pen floods out facts
and fictions gleaned from newspaper stacks
where swamp rats nest;
his treatise transmutes in the dusk
into letters unsent to the women
who once walked his hill,
and hearing the Furies amassing
their treetop forces,
he singes the bellicose dark
with his kerosene aura,
calling the stillness home –
calling the stillness
home.

Thunderdown Gondwana

Cascade the melting mountain,
drown the Lost World Caves;
gush down Myrtle Gully,
where Antarctic tree ferns quiver;
flood sassafras and leatherwood,
and stands of silver wattle
where snow whirls bubble wildly
in blackberry-bunkered springs.
Roar at the city
that you wash the bones of Gondwana,
and we suckle its thunderblood.

Inglewood Road, Cascades

Uphill from the converted schoolhouse,
a donkey clops through freckles of forget-me-nots
to sniff my empty fingers at the fence-line.
I stroke her yoke-stained back,
wondering if Simpson's name-forgotten donkey
might have hauled through cannon fire
some shredded boy turned digger
by this schoolhouse.

A fanfare rolls
dolorously from the Organ Pipes,
heralding the Theatre of War
of this new century,
where narcosis, sloth or halitosis
will not besmirch the honour of old dead men,
or our fallen youth in Bali.

Greenlings erupt in the stone-scorched earth.
Wind rips through treetops
saved from last year's smouldering
by the shaving of the fire trail.

Antipodean May Day

A mercurial grey
sucks in the first dawn bleeding;
gold spears of light
combust in a cloudburn
as the dancers spring
through the tattering winds of winter.

They bell out their double steps
to the bird trills of flageolets,
the lung beat of bellows,
the sword clash of hawthorn,
then waver like moths, soft
to the sawing of fiddles,
and look down from the dolmens
at a piercing of church spires,
knowing they're cuckoos
laying their paradoxes
in the nest-spin of far older magics.

Fishing For Stars, Tiananmen Square, 2001

I

Within this Gate of Heavenly Peace
the only stars are fixed five-pointers,
Red Army neon in a greenhouse sky dome.
Streetlights balance loftily
like descended space craft shining.
Gold filigrees of lighted pearls
drape temple roofs and august walls.
From the Forbidden City
Mao's expansive presence beams.

The obelisk to the People's Heroes
illuminates the inner Square;
grey-stone statues build
the new Great Wall under enemy fire;
sentries stand with rifles barbed,
waiting for the enemy to be named.

White-gloved soldiers march
mechanically past Mao's shrine
where thousands shuffle to grieve
that crystal light embalmed,
apotheosised, yet slowly decomposing.

Hawkers deal in operatic lines,
and in this breath of summer night
the masses now are flying kites.

But my refractory line of masks
won't pivot and swing with t'ai chi grace.
The commander of my gang of four
won't quell the insurrection of his back row boys
with that fixed red scowling.
Perhaps they sense a lack
of discipline in foreign fingers.

II

Students practise charm in English,
preserving alien images
in camera clicks and flashes.
Children propel themselves like bees,
hunched and helmeted in line,
with clockwise whirrs of roller blades
on concrete tiles. They would not have seen
the tanks out here, grinding down dissenters' bone,
but do their nights nurse dreams
of immolation?

III

Dragon wings unfold,
silk-bright in expectancy.
Radiant in Olympic favour,
slums make way for movie sets
as the dragon marries her young
in black and white
and sends them off to suited futures.
I follow a gossamer thread of sight
to the fading gleam of a flying fish.
Within this Gate of Heavenly Peace,
the old master demonstrates
with consummate ease his handline skill.
Surpassing all this ground-lit glory,
he fishes the zenith
for enlightenment.

Aeroplane Awakening

I was in an alchemy of light,
a witness to the sacred tincturing
of mystic mounds and waves
that might have been sastrugi ice
as the sky intoned its ritual of tangerine,
maroon and violet vestments swirling,
sparking all that vaporous iron
to a coin of molten gold.

The passenger beside me stirred.
I tensed, knowing words
could shatter this enchantment,
while the trite sentence,
'look, it's sunrise,' dragged me back
to a cramped, metallic cell of time,
hurtling towards a waking city
on a reckless descent from eternity.

Old Farm Road

I steal jonquils from an unkempt plot
where a sawn-off trunk of blue gum
spikes the tray of an abandoned truck,
surrounded by its sapling progeny.

No mechanical cacophonies.
No hare-lipped beggars working
temple gates or New World centres,
no thousand jostling smells and voices,
just the idling of Depression history
and cadences of magpie calls.

I drink peace from an untamed creek
then take my floral tribute home,
dunk it in a carafe of water
and call this *spring*,
and call this being home.

Weedy Sea Dance

Surging from a rocky cloister,
a ruby knight pursues his prey
in ragged drifts
through a seagrass meadow.
Close by a red queen loiters,
intent on tangling
with this fearsome hunter.

A seek and chase begins
with sea fronds dangling.
A flaunted reel,
a see-saw joust,
then yellow dots
bind purple bars,
until the final fire-burst of frenzy,
when the queen spawns her pearls
in a silver of fingerlings.

Unravelling their connubial knot,
the queen departs with gangling grace,
no backward look at her smug knave,
subsiding to his weed-bright sea bed.

His prize now sealed in swelling tail cups,
he snorts his fill of hapless mysids,
for in this sunken looking glass realm
a pregnant squire requires his sustenance.

Iceberg

Launched
dawn-stained
in a churn of sea ice,
this glacial maiden sails
the krill-red waves
and sea mists
pregnant with the souls
of long dead mariners
drowning on some pirate longline.

Lugubrious
in her north-by-easting,
she chills cetacean songlines
until, cradled on a graveyard reef,
the ageing majesty unbinds her stays,
cackling at the crosswinds
those pristine pocks
of air-time trapped
when humans first tamed fire
or learnt to read their journeys by the stars.

Bass Strait Sealers

This cove has the breath of scarred sea lions,
the salt-lick brush of raw wounds, iron-gripped mussels
that erode the granite boulders to the nerve,
a haunting of violation, fragile as shards of nautilus.

The sealers had become patriarchs
by the time the bishop's clinker scraped ashore.
They begged respectability,
Christian weddings to their wifeys,
baptisms for their children.
They vowed to build a schoolhouse
if the Church would provide a teacher,
and all hands could go at this together.
But they were never grateful for education
since that meant being herded off their islands,
rounded up to be flocked and fleeced.

Those women they dragged here
skinned the horizon with handspike eyes,
smoking out familiar voices from Wybalenna,
on that badland island, where their sisters sang
their childless grievings; and in the dredging
of their shell-laced breasts by coppery kids,
all smiles and two-tongued jibberings,
they pierced the flimsy shells of memory,
knuckling themselves to unmiddened futures.

Those pools of crystal salt could fix your eyes
and drown you in a moonbird rising.

An Unknown Wreck, Macquarie Island

There calmly let him sleep.
Not all the winds that blow
Can shake his bed, and he shall keep
A quiet watch below.

Chief harpooner, Henry Whalley, squinted
at the frozen headland as the feeble day
foundered in a clobber of hailstones.
Other ships had broken backs on this saw-blade island coastline,
and Whalley might have heard above those cut-throat winds,
voices bellowing to the rocking darkness
that such violent seas as these could have no origin in Christendom,
but the demented fury of the Old World sea gods.

Sparks sprayed and shrieked
in the manic shuntings of the iron traveller.
A volcanic belch erupted in a red hiss of stove steam.
Invisible hands unfurled the jibs
to jabber and vaunt like ghosts,
while a skeleton hand of lightning
pointed shorewards to the shingle.

Thunder over-rolled the Master's orders.
Cables jerked and dragged the folded sea bed
until a comber, foaming high as heaven,
dumped its avalanche of silence.
Desperate oaths and prayers surfaced
in a swirl of splintered bone and rigging.

Seals hauled ashore to pulse and wallow
around kelp-strung wreckage,
and when the melting morning
was kited with skua and great petrel,
swooping to gobble the bright spoils of the storm,
a rope line of men shuffled barefoot from the breakers,
then shepherded their wounded
along the icy foreshore.

In a weather-torn sealers' hut,
Whalley gulped a warm, salty coffee,
sighed and slipped to an endless sleep,
where he might have seen his frozen-bearded father
eyeing the right whale's spume
while his mother surged to surface
like a seal among sea rocks.

When the castaways dug Whalley's grave,
their iron struck wood, deep in the shingle,
exposing the ribs of an older wreck
which had carried unknown mariners
from an unknown country,
across all known frontiers.
Mist drifted on the storm-stilled ocean,
draped its numbing peace around the island,
then retreated to another Eden,
untouched as yet by New World harpoons.

The epitaph of Tasmanian Aboriginal whaler, Henry Whalley, which prefaces this poem, is quoted from J.S. Thomson, 1912, *Voyages and Wanderings in Far Off Lands and Seas*.

Bellerive's Old Fort

I hoist you to the cannon mound
where you, my father, lifted me,
once in a time that bobs like blubber
on this whaleback-walking river.

My hand skin wears its own map of experience
but yours is translucent,
a palimpsest of skin and vein and bone,
the toddler's hand –
you caught diphtheria on the voyage out,
and nearly didn't make Fremantle;
the schoolboy's hand –
nuns crowed delight at your Irish lilt
and made you say the Hail Mary solo;
the soldier's hand that tapped Morse code in Lei;
the hand that tailored suits for forty years
then retired to do the washing up.

We scan the estuary for a hostile slice of flying jibs,
t'gallants, cannoned decks –
The menace remains, my brother observes,
only its name and livery changes.

We dig shards of memory from this site,
the ramblings of your Sunday tribe
loosed from morning Mass to piss-dank tunnels.
We shrieked delighted terror
when you sang that graveyard song.
My brother remembers me running away,
leaving him lost and frightened.
I remember being trapped in cells
wherever my brothers could find them
on this island of iron bars.

Our mother finds no recollections here.
She sees the bastion afresh,
ghosts banished by the sandblasting.
A tended picnic ground. Notices erected.
Not the wild and weedy ruin we romped in.
Then we realise she was always left at home
to nurse her pregnancies or latest baby,
reconstructing with collapsing walls
an order to our chaos.

I wait for Hamlet's apparition
on the brink of this amphitheatre,
opining of things undreamt of by my family,
tarred corpses hanging on Hunter Island,
smoky questions that rise above the mountain,
those mountain-dark eyes accuse us still.

On the way home you fall against the kerb,
graze your delicate scalp,
and your nose drips,
blood-red as any turnkey,
          turncoat,
                    redcoat's jacket.

Buckley Under the Playground

The plump nest of a child's palm yields a hieroglyph,
a curlicue of flaking rust, edged to surface
by the soil's decadence.
Children careen, hoop balls, pound bitumen,
dodge, catch, chatter,
muffling secrets that vibrate
like a hollow log coffin
with its aura of insects droning.

There've been television grabs,
a campaign to champion
that six-foot-four-inch clod of clay,
invoke him as the new Ned Kelly,
Reconciliation's father,
to exhume and box those long, long Cheshire bones,
return them to their rightful place.

The Wada Wurrung land?
Geelong?

Octogenarians recall the grim magnetic pull
of a graveyard where the school is now,
A giant's tombstone teeth,
Weathered etchings of fore-shortened lives.
One of them remembers bones.
Dug up. Carted away. Some time.
Some bones? His? Who's left to know?

And who would want to tell the children
their school is built on a graveyard?
Why muddy educational clarity
with talk of languages lost
with the damming of time streams?
Or tell them braided stories
with fish trap nets of meaning
and kinship webs unwoven?

Why unmanacle that jumped-up dead man,
who haunted the Wada Wurrung children
and would not recoil into camp smoke
even in the sunshocked mornings,
for he might again exact his toll for carriageway
by stampeding a million cloven hoofs
across a thousand dreamlines?

Long may such irksome notions rest
with Buckley's bones, Buckley's hope
and Buckley's chance,
beyond return,
beyond oblivion.

In the staff room
the coffin handle is named,
then binned.

Spiritlands Undreaming

I

Two decades' worth of miracles
jumbled into trunks and cases,
I step down from the thundered air.
Red naga'd boys stand brolga-legged
to greet the week's supplies.

My schoolroom hunkers
on a numinous plane.
Oppression smoulders, iron hot.
In the kinder caravan,
the air conditioner's broken.
Clots of cumulonimbus bruise
the sky above the burnt-out plane,
supersaturated with prophecies
of fecundity amidst decay.

A tympani of thunder
beats a ceremonial prelude.
First season's laughter. First rain.

My class decamps from writing work,
discarding lessons with shorts and dresses,
to join with tangling limbs and shrieking,
the chorus of the rain-danced earth.
The movement storms towards its climax.
First rain.

II

Like ibises of the billabong
we teachers watch from stilted heights.
Children bathe in cut-down petrol drums
while women recycle sit-down money
with the chance logic of their cards.

We sit with you, the children say, we play school.
We've played school all day, I say.

Some educrats asked the wrong people
where to build the school.
They built on sacred ground,
and then, they say, old people died.

Exotic ways advance like cane toads.
Devils drive Toyotas,
turtlemen flap vampire capes.
We find a rifle in the mangroves
its wood decayed, its danger cold.

III

Your grandmother's on the trampoline,
says the little night bird
after the gift of my skin's naming.
In the wall-less cathedral of nights,
bloodless rites of birth and death
are beat in ceremonies of Aussie Rules and Morning Star.

Apostasy begins its sliding through sediments of myth and time.
Farewell, the keepers of the fire, blood, bone, bread and fire,
weave them into arcane hatchings of spirit space and kinship time.

IV

This mosquito net's a shadow screen,
abandoned by the teacher I replaced;
he was given a day to get out or be speared,
for the girl was promised.
They upset the order.

A policeman shoots his rage
above humpies,
over houses
to the stars.

Waves beat a steady rhythm
to the raucous mudflat chorus
of the tendril-tangled night.

V

Boys smear clay masks on their foreheads,
dive and swim the serpentining river,
swim crocodile.
A rough-barked head rears in the mangroves
and a spirit light ascends
to the stars.

Fifteenth Summer

His hair coppercurls in all this shimmering,
his bony shoulders broaden.
He calls;
his father's voice doesn't fit him yet.
I scan the bull kelp blotches on the seabed.

Last night I floated in such a dream as this
while he lunged and parried
some poisoned barb,
slashed and shivered
until a disembodied voice announced,
your baby boy is dead.
But he's here still, straining,
not yet swung loose from his holdfast.

A sea eagle returns to her cliff face calling
to shelter her fat fledgling
above the eyrie edge of time.
A cloaked darkness skates the bay,
its scimitar slices darkly.
I sidestep its imagined arc.

Seventeenth Winter

Nibs of marram grass
scribble onto rain-pocked sand
as our footsteps breach uncertain gaps
between yesterday and tomorrow.

The boy no longer walks
beside his sister or his mother.
He stands in a distant break of boobiallas,
reading the sandbar's barrelling,
revisiting the bay
he's left behind for shark-finned curlers,
scanning nebulous futures
that whorl around him
in an opalescent flush
of abalone shell or sunset.

It's as if this earlobe bay
is listening too,
whispering his provenance,
whispering his providence.

Valuing

I was bare-ankled in the bracken
when he called, hunting for saplings
to transplant along the fence-line,
until I discovered all those olive featherings
were tapped in a single root.
To sever one could mean the death of all.
I know it's hard, he says, I see this all the time.

I think of children begging car keys,
chugging the paddock to Great Oyster Bay,
the sacerdotal rites of hooded dotterels,
beached fleets of jellied moonlets,
titanic moons that rear above Ile des Phoques,
ponderous echidnas which, like him,
inspect my drying dam,
and wonder, as he paces boundaries,
how he'll spool location (and location and location)
into a strangling cord of dollars
that divides into loss.

Watch out for snakes,
he kindly warns before he leaves.

Secateurs

The carpet bares its scars like war wounds.
Cobwebs etch the shaky silhouettes
of missing clutter.

I twist through the dusty window frame
to stem the advance of grape vines
which clog drains and downpipes
with veined hands grasping.
There's nurturing in cutting back.

No piano now, no plug-in music.
My fat dog sits, mesmerised
by the secateurs' slicing.
She would have gone too, the old bitch.
We understand each other
implicitly.

The Beginning of Wonders, Marakoopa

I

The moon presides upon these snow-capped tiers,
a shadow past her luminous climax.
Such bold attraction should defy Earth's gravity,
yet my weighted tread alarms.

Fences impose linearity
upon the fractals of this remnant forest.
Barns hunker into karst in assorted states of entropy.
Pasture erodes to sinkholes.
Sinkholes collapse to helictite dungeons.

I pass an old swamp gum,
chainsawed to the shape of a tuning fork.
Skull-faced Herefords uproot and masticate
a skin of pasture, scabrous with limestone.
A wallaby sounds a subterranean well.
Fence wires twang like a loose-stringed guitar.

A decaying barn is shouldered by a brick dunny
and a flashy shed of corrugated steel.
A pelmet of saffron cloth adorns its open doorway.
Unberried brambles reach hands inside,
as if trying to strangle ghosts.

That knoll could be hollowed in cruciform,
a womb, a pleasure dome, a tomb
for families who left tools and bones
by a watershed cave whose mouth speaks divinations
in a language we will not learn.

In this biosphere of art and science,
imagination bears down upon an age-old geomancy
and whichever way you look at it,
this is enchantment.

II

I will not rise before the frost departs
and superb blue wrens come bouncing back
to the mission-brown deck of this ranger's hut.

Chocolate-wattled bats crickle in the ceiling.
One visits my bunk,
flaunts its fighter-pilot skills.
The bats are like creeks around here
in their curious vanishments and resurgences.

III

In the cave mouth known as Beginning of Wonders
moisture strains through limestone straws
to build stalactites, stalagmites and columns,
while quixotic spins sculpt palm trees and pilgrims,
shawls and organ pipes,
the nativity scene in the Great Cathedral.

This morning, in the glow worm chamber,
a cave guide told how a couple first kissed
when he flicked off the spotlights.
They'll soon be wed in the glowworm chamber.
He drew down darkness
and the punters gasp orgasmically
in that subterranean mirror of the stars.

IV

Tonight's moon is veiled in widow-black.
A satellite blinks, blue as the burning excreta
of fungus gnat pupae.

Passing a half-pink cottage,
scaffolded for its spring greening,
I see a couple entwined behind glass.
They stare accusingly.
Perhaps they do not know I am ephemeral.
I could be walking on moonmilk tunnels,
rim pool pearls and floating islands.
They do not know I am,
I am… I am… Echo.

By the River Alph, which burbles
out of the Kubla Khan Cave,
a pregnant cloud has fallen to Earth.
Caught in the attraction and repulsion
of the Underworld, I know a fear as old
as Fear itself. Through the howling of the dogs of war
I hear the music of a distant dulcimer
and cry for peace,
and the forsaking of a demon lover.

Through Paradise, Running On Empty

Mole Creek's only servo shuts at noon on Saturdays
and the next bowser's the other side of Paradise.
Motoring off in a tickertape parade of autumn leaves,
vermilion, gold, carmine, I cross the Union bridge –
best place to see a platypus on the Mersey River.
I pass a plantation of sapling *E. globulus*
with khaki-skirts and waxed blue petticoats –
their uniformity defies the natural disorder.
A sudden shock of mountain
has been sliced away to a limekiln.
A sawmill's grinding logs to dusty cones.
Winter sun slides off the giant mountains,
Roland and Claude.
An eastern barred bandicoot lies,
brain-mashed on the bitumen.
A log truck labours upwards.
I strain behind it, stuck between second
and third gears, not daring to pass on these windings.
Forestry signs welcome visitors to the Gog Range,
declaring this a working forest –
working like a woman chained,
shaved, burnt, ploughed, and seeded.

On my tank-filled return from Sheffield
the bandicoot's leg is raised in a rigor mortis salute
to the passing of feather, wing and claw,
and I'm back to Mole Creek in a deciduous blaze,
having fed the air with CO_2 and seen the rape of Paradise.

Devil's Lookout

We grind upwards through the re-gen forest,
headlights battering at the fog,
then pull up by druidic boulders,
walk the duckboard to the Devil's Lookout
and stand beneath a lava flow of cloud,
suspended in the sunrise.

They give the Devil's name
to natural forms that beggar belief,
and there's much of that around here.
So many of his parts are named:
the Devil's Gullet, Earhole, Drainpipe,
the Devil's Anastomosis.

In high winds, my guide has had to pull back tourists
from this edge, for lives these days are so safely railed
some have no fear of the Devil's mischief.

Our gaze banks above bluffs, the nanatuck,
Mount Pelion East and West, Mt Ossa,
hovers above the Fisher Power Scheme,
clear-fell in the Fisher Valley,
Man's affront to the Devil's grandeur,
ingesting the wild like the devil's tumour.

Small Expectations

The lagoon has drained and flooded
since I took you to my sanctum.
We opened portals to our souls
and words rattled out like felons fleeing.

We launched our coracle in such gentle lapping.
Since then, tyrant winds have lashed
the headland blowhole high,
confounding expectations
that there would be no shadow
of another parting.

Seeking the Alpha Male

The chimp has taken up smoking,
spitting at gawkers with shadow-striped faces.
A zoo psychologist diagnoses sexual frustration,
but not for lack of suitable offers.
This simian starlet was raised away
from the natural order
and has designs above her station.
She wants to meet her psychologist's clan,
go to movies, raves and dinner parties,
dreams sultry nights in his jungle kitchen;
and for one transferring moment,
he ponders Sigmund Freud and B.F. Skinner,
Homo habilis and *Homo erectus*,
and why a two per cent genetic variance
should justify the bars that lock him out.

Domestos

Where are her champions
in this Chaos of Postmodernity?
Blood bright chieftains who would thwart
the watchdog at those wrought iron gates
and reclaim her as their queen or goddess;
young men and old, who once would have given gold,
or more, for the minted brush of her breath,
and even in rejection, would protect
her tainted honour with their death?

Only Ajax stands her ally now,
laying waste bacterial legions
he spins, demented in the vortex
wherein her passion chills.

Her kitchen coruscates in the emptiness of morning,
her wrinkling mirror image leers.
Could some new potion, cream or scalpel
repair to alabaster brightness
her fading charms, and even then,
would that restore the ardour of her champions?

Whitegoods hum their mockery
at her caricature of beauty.
Soon she'll spray her chemical weapons down
on crumpled sheets and underwear.
She's in control with aerosol, and a little covert gin,
but where are Helen's champions now?

Interview

He could have been any Inquisitor,
Grand or otherwise,
immigration official, lover, serial killer,
or head of department (acting),
his gaze a flick knife of enticements
that he dangled
then denied.

And she?
A rag doll, perhaps,
the one she cut, stuffed,
and embroidered the mouth
to an inscrutable smile
with the unravelling hem
of her grandmother's dress –
the birthday present
for her missing daughter.

Sphinx Rock

Below the organ pipes
but above the realm of eagles,
a baby's ashes ride this turbulence,
speckling the waratah he never saw,
and try as she might,
his mother will not conceive again.

I do not phone the dead to talk to you,
and yet as I sit above this harbour,
watching silver trunks sway
like the masts of bygone barques,
I explore the aching marrow of your absence,
knowing that at your age
I would have made your choices.

Great Oyster Bay Before a Storm

Ile des Phoques sails an indigo sea,
always ahead on its error of parallax;
ridged clouds, like eroded blades of cuttlefish,
are blotting up the sunset.
Ahead, I see a pink form on sand,
a mermaid perhaps, or another woman murdered
in this east coast paradise.
A thunderhead is rising from the headland.

I stop to inspect a beached white pointer,
young, just a metre long,
its coin eye half-closed,
gill slits deathly grey.

Running on towards the ragged sleeve of Freycinet,
I turn at the rocks, and in a tumble of an hourglass,
upend myself in time.
I could be crossing tracks of women
with string bags knocking with mussels
and turban shells as they drag children's hands
to the safety of campfires,
the thunder and lightning dance
and the fleshy warmth of bark shelters.
Pied oystercatchers are running too,
stamping convict arrows
on the sand's last golden glow.

Ile des Phoques floats behind me now,
its wild men shooting and clubbing,
rendering seals in try pots,
decanting oil for lamplight.
Tonight, who knows how
they'll keep their slippery foothold
on that guano-white rock?

Maria Island swims into view like a giant nautilus.
The convict, Alexander Miller,
has stowed aboard the *Caroline*,
bound for southern sealing.
After a year of subantarctic tempests,
he'll beg the treadmill and Maria's temperate shelter.
William Smith O'Brien is out there now.
Too much the Irish gentleman for shackles,
he'll abuse his privileges
with the gaol governor's daughter.
God-beams stream from a bloodied sky.

A squadron of herons flies in on steely wings
to land in a tremulus of kangaroo grass.
Soon my hermitage will creak and moan
like an ark in a deluge,
but until the glass has spun again
I'll not yet feel the ineluctable rip
that will drag my soul away,
or know how many king tides must pass
before I will raise my pen to the wind again.

Pilgrimage, 1980

Dublin, it's making me old, you are,
and turning my black hairs grey,
your satirical mould and smoke-fired cold
are eating my lungs away,
choking me and your burr-haired children
and your motley old prophets as well.
I burnt my poems before I came away
but they're rising bright in a fever.
A Celtic twilight passes with heroes and martyrs
through peeling patterns of wallpaper.

Time, when this scorching is cold
to travel north to the border,
where hope foments in blood-gold chalices
and whispered fears are sipped
and belched as scornful laughter.
Time to visit the store where my father was born,
the graveyard where wee uncle Rogie lies,
old neighbours who recall the auction day
when my grandparents sold and moved away
lest their children be bled in the Troubles.
Time, where impassioned pleas for peace are still heard
in the blazings of outrageous fires
in the burnished minds of zealots and liars
as they did in scarce remembered days
when my family fled for Tasmania,
a mission land, so far, so safe from the border.

The Calliag

My cousin shows me his farm in South Armagh.
We're a stone's throw from the Republic
and he's delighted I've come home,
a generation after being born away.

Slieve Gullion looms above us,
woodland green, volcanic grey.
There's a small lake at the summit,
Calliag Bheara's Lough, the Lake of Sorrow,
the calliag being a witch or hag.
There are cairns up there,
one a megalithic passage grave, forty-foot long.
I think of our ancestors' DNA
spiralling through my bones.

Looking down the road to Dromintee
we speak of hedge schools, of ragged children
and defiant teachers, and the vagrant my father
used to tell us about. Seeing clothes hung to dry
on a hedge, he'd beg, bush will you swap?
Taking silence for assent, he'd help himself
and leave his rags swinging.

So the famine hit hard around here, I say.
Och aye, my cousin replies, people had to pay
twelve pounds a year or two pigs to absent landlords
who'd wine, dine and grow fat on the profits.

Those landlords turned whole families out of cottages.
Och aye, even widder women and childer
starved wandering this road. But after an eviction
there was always a woman in the village who'd curse the land
so no crops would grow, and a whole generation would pass
before smoke would rise from the chimneys again.
Och aye, he says, I'm delighted you've come home.

The Gap

Hawthorn borders the field we're standing in.
Knuckled and autumnal, it's still flaring green
in a varnish of sunlight.

Your grandfather and my father planted that hedge,
my cousin explains, but they needed more quicks.
Quicks? I ask.
Och aye, young sticks of hawthorn.
Y'r grandfather said he'd buy them in the village
and come back and plant them,
but he took his family to Tasmania instead.

I stare at my grandfather's unfinished business;
the height of this eighty-four year old hedge
is the span of my father's life in Australia.
Then I recall my father saying often,
'I'll be back.'

Mickey Fadgy's Ulster

My cousin shows us down a cow lane
with a row of disused cottages
to The Pad, where cousins
of various degrees of removal
grew themselves up.
I ask if the cousins might come back.
Och, I shouldn't think so, he replies.
Some of them had brains to burn, you know.

He shows us our ancestral cottage,
whitewashed stone, trimmed with maroon,
an iron stove, two rooms,
no electricity or running water.

The bedroom has a loft built by my grandfather
when he was only twelve.
And isn't it as good now as the day he built it?
There are creeping holes in the Irish oak planking,
but we admire the handiwork anyway.

Then he tells us about the coat.
Upturning a plastic bucket left over
from his last refurbishment,
I stand and peer aloft,
and there it is, dangling from nail in a rafter,
Micky Fadgy's ulster, shoulders padded with swallow shit.
And isn't it as good as the day he left it there?

We hoist ten-year-old nephew to the loft.
He crosses and re-crosses rickety boards
and hands down the coat.
Ah, you're a hero, we say.

The coat was finely crafted in its day.
Double breasted before its thread began to rot.
A swallow-tail, my cousin says,
although the swallow has lost some feathers.

I thrust my arms through its sleeves
dreading scorpions and spiders,
and know it has held its warmth for a hundred years.
My nephew dons his great-great-grandfather's coat
and it swallows him up.
Puffing his chest, he grins beneath his baseball cap.

Later, in his farmhouse,
our cousin shows us a newspaper clipping,
an article about a trial presided over by the magistrate cousin.
Och aye, he says, I shouldn't think they'd be comin' back.

Busking Angel, Perth

It must have been the season for angels.
They were raining from clouds,
buzzing around like blowflies, winging out of films
and prayer books, petrifying in graveyards
or being taken in by new age retailers,
with their angel cards and angel healings,
so it should have come as no surprise
that I met one in the mall
the day I drove in from the east.

She magnetised, this fallen angel.
Children placed propitiations at her feet
while I stood wondering whether the silver monotone
of her face, gown, hair and wings
was more disconcerting than her immobility.
Then she caught the tremor
of my soul and beckoned me.

I've had messages enough from angels
to last three life times, I pleaded in dumbshow.
But her eyes impressed the gelatin of my retinas
and, for fear she would take flight within my skull
and invade my very being,
I yielded my widow's mite.
Then she sprinkled me with angel dust
and a silent welcome to the west.

Rules For Living In a Postbox

There is always light at the back of the tunnel.
>Look forward,
>not back,
>or regret will blind you.

Wait for the key's turning.
>There are chinks
>in the citadel of half-truths,
>you don't need to cast arrows.

Ride the night air
>let the moon be your beacon
>Your bicycle is the next best thing to a broomstick.

National Poetry Week

The Prime Minister once declared
that by the year 2000 no Australian poet
would be living in poverty,
and, Wonderwoman that she is,
she's kept her word,
so we poets all have dinky jobs
with time out for writing,
readings, book tours and signings,
holidays abroad for inspiration
or as therapy for writers' block.

And now the Les Murray Stadium
is full to bursting.
Punters have been camping
out for days, scalpers scalping.

We poets have trained for this festival,
sharpened our irony, buffed up our metaphors,
fine-tuned rhythm, consonance, assonance,
rhymes and half-rhymes, but we know that what will win
through in the end is the sheer, raw passion of words
that bump, pinch, punch, grind, gouge and bruise,
ideas that blaze and amaze.
Complacency comes easily, but in some other universe,
who knows? We could be reading poetry
to empty chairs in the mall.

Wildflower Show, King's Park

For V.H.

It's been a year
        since you clacked the spoons
           to the Mucky Duck's beat
                and had the children up
                      and whirring this green,
                      like petals in soft tornado.

It's been six months since that violet film
              showed how far the crab
                  had crept inside your breast
                  to nest within your marrow.

Magpies strut this bed of kangaroo paws
        as they did last year,
               and the thundering sky refracts your
memory,
                        red,

                            orange

                                  yellow

                                                    blue

                                  indigo

                            violet
    as the river bears you away
                to the Indian Ocean,
                        fading to white, grey,
                        moving, misting.

Bread Upon the Waters, Lake Jualbup

Tortoises crossing, a road signs caution;
an ancient shellback hangs in the shallows,
bearing not the earth upon his shell
but a forest of algae;
skinflaking,
      still.
            Too still.

Swans promenade in pairs
or scroll the lake like Viking longboats.
A ragged stump of swan is dredging depths
where her mate floats limply.

Other signs warn us not to feed the wildlife.
We think botulism is killing them,
a council workman says,
people feed them and they stay
instead of heading off to purer waters.
He buries five tortoises, puts a cross on their graves.

This man maintains the fountains,
tiles unruly edges, yet the mortar
still preserves the graffiti, *fuck*,
as if the wildlife needed a reminder.
In the shrubbing of that handmade island
swans brood away from human eyes
but tortoises attack the cygnets.
Eat frail webbed legs.

Three girls hunker at the lake's edge,
face-pierced adolescents, about your age,
chewing white bread rolls.
Eurasian coots skitter,
red-eyed and mendicant,
leaving wakes of Pyrrhic victory.
Those girls have read the signs
but like you, have not yet learned
that charming waters can brew toxicity.

Summer's glowering makes feathered bones.
It's not just wildlife we can love to death.

Statue of the Arts, Albany

Between the windowless shed that was once a morgue
and the glassed-in deck of the old nurses' quarters,
a girl brandishes a recorder
while dancing on an artist's palette,
her movement stilled in die-cast bronze;
and I wonder what the ghosts think
of the winged frottage of honeyeater
that hovers above, around, beneath her lifting skirt.
Do they twitter invisible tongues
at her scant attire and pubescent nipples,
wanting to confine such revelations
to the sick, the dead or the shamed?
Or do they rejoice in shedding veils
and trip-length uniforms,
willing the bird to taste their honey?

Villanelle For Miranda

Those pink arcs above your eyes should not be there,
the mortician's handiwork, not your own. Should
I take a lock from your new-styled hair?

Beneath this sheet your skin is bare, marked
only by the seat belt's scar. Your pain, my child, is now my own.
Those pink arcs above your eyes should not be there.

You lived and loved intensely, dared to dare. Like
a fledgling swift, you were leaving home. Should
I take a lock from your new-styled hair?

You incandesced with joy and care.
Does your spirit hover or has it flown? Those pink arcs
above your eyes should not be there.

Questions rise on sterile air.
No answers fall from frozen lips. Should
I take a lock from your new-styled hair?

Shouldn't I, dear girl, be lying there,
an empty hull of flesh and bone?
Those pink arcs above your eyes should not be there.
Should I take a lock from your new-styled hair?

Inheritance

The elation
of your last goodbye.

Childish scribble
on the wall of memory:
I love you, Mummy.

A crack
moving at glacial speed
through the cup you left behind.

Butterfly Road

I have received many gifts of butterflies.
At Pinaroo, boxes of monarchs
were presented to your next of kin –
mine settled,
lowered its wings on my heart chakra
and rested for eighteen-year-long seconds,
before blessing the open sore of your grave
and the grief-bowed heads of your friends.

Butterflies followed me south and east,
flying before my walks around Gordon's Hill,
luring me on to belief, then transforming
into dry gum leaves.

There have been other butterflies:
in Melbourne, a chance gift of a book,
an illustrated Chaos Theory for children;
a butterfly found in my brother-in-law's van
after I'd been a passenger,
and he's not into transformational symbols,
messages from beyond the grave,
or anything beyond the world as he knows it.

On summer days, butterflies drift

Hermitage Road, flutter red and white correa
or batter the glass of my cottage
and I lie awake grappling with synchronicity,
Rorschaching pine knots on the ceiling,
stamping meaning onto random forms
until I decide it doesn't matter
how many hidden dimensions I want you to inhabit
or how many alternative realities I invent
to treat the weeping ulcer of your loss,
for every the beat of a butterfly's wings
is the kick of your foetal feet in my womb,
a pulse in the umbilical cord
that binds us still.

Learning To Love Fragments

For twenty months now,
each day has been an island
borne away to the void
by the grizzled surf of night.

On sunny days I hear echoes
of you playing
with your brother and cousin
in the sand dunes
They say this beach is a healing place.

I sit in my cottage writing up a sea mist,
and when I climb the stile
to Great Oyster Bay
the beach is occluded.

I write back to the day
when I should have rung your mobile,
asked how are you were going.
Found work yet? Where are you staying?
Enjoying yourself? Love you, darling.
A few seconds' delay
and you would not have been at that place
at that exact time.
The truck would have passed safely.

I walk the beach with downcast eyes, remembering
the cowry you held out to me. You knew the value
of the world's first currency before I did.
I used to wonder if you'd been here before.
Now I wish I'd learned more from you.

Sometimes I collect shells.
I take them home to my windowsill,
but their power blanches in the sun,
reminding me to keep your memory
glistening between tides.

I see cowries where you discovered yours,
in loose white sand where the sea bursts
through the channel and pools in the lagoon.
Often I see bones, their marrow bleached to lace work,
decay transformed to beauty

I stoop to inspect fans of doughboy scallops,
marvelling at the way a fractal fan
angles out of the parent's hinge,
their whole and the part are equal casualties
to the remorselessness of time and tide.
Your childhood and your single week of adulthood
has now become your whole.
I see you in the quarter moon,
your unlived life as unlit lunar territory,
as present as your absence.
Once I stooped to perfection
now I am learning to love fragments.
Cutaways of whelk and helmet shells,
their exposed spirals drilling down
to wherever it is that you are now.

I seek your face in abalone shells
upturned to the sunset,
although their jagged edges wound and scar.
I feel you as a phantom limb,
a lopped-off branch of my family tree
that creaks and bleeds in a wind-rushed gully.

They say this beach is a healing place,
and as the grizzled surf of night
bears each day away to the void,
I hold the fragment of your life in mine,
the happy mischief of a ragged smile.

The Sweetening Shadows

The smell of plum jam
trespasses
through memory's
aching corners.

Evening ripples
ruffle
the polish
of heavy-metal waters.

Sweetness rides quicksilver
the salted winds
of the estuary.

Next night again
the sugared darkness
breathes.

Anne Morgan was born in Tasmania and has recently returned from Western Australia to live on the slopes of Mount Wellington. She holds a Master of education from the University of Tasmania and a PhD in Writing from Edith Cowan University (ECU), for which she won a university medal. She is currently an honorary postdoctoral fellow of ECU.

She has taught in Tasmania, the Northern Territory and China. She has also worked as a professional actor (far too briefly) and as a public servant (for far too long). She currently writes full-time, across several genres. She is the author of six published children's books including the Captain Clawbeak series (Random House Australia).

Her website address is www.annemorgan.com.au

www.ingramcontent.com/pod-product-compliance
Lightning Source LLC
Chambersburg PA
CBHW062151100526
44589CB00014B/1791

Colleen Keating
Desert Patterns

Dedication

To our grandchildren, Lachlan, Thomas, Tyler, Jacinta, Cameron, Edison, Dominic, Eleanor, Gemma, Darcy and Ethan and their burgeoning love for this country.

Desert Patterns
ISBN 978 1 76041 844 1
Copyright © text Colleen Keating 2020
Cover photo by Praewthida K on Unsplash

First published 2020 by
GINNINDERRA PRESS
PO Box 3461 Port Adelaide 5015 Australia
www.ginninderrapress.com.au

Contents

Introduction	9
Dadirri	10
The Top End of Australia	
in the beginning	13
crew	14
blank page	15
a grand sweep of landscape	16
this is not alien land	17
Kakadu	18
the Jesus bird	19
parallel realms	20
cicada dreaming	21
Nitmiluk	22
Kununurra	25
Yellow Water Billabong	26
Gibb River Road	27
Litchfield National Park 1	28
Litchfield National Park 2	29
seeking permission	30
mystery of Munurru	31
touch this earth	32
Geikie Gorge	34
Mabel Downs Station	35
brahmins buddhas boabs	36
Purnululu National Park	37
Bungle Bungles	38
Jandamarra 1	40
Jandamarra 2	41
Jandamarra 3	43
closed full stop	44

cathedrals pyramids and buddhas	45
from the bus	47
Broome	48
ponderings	49
mulga dreaming	50
desert patterns	51
bush tucker	53
desert domes	55
at Rabbits Flat	56
Uluru	57
the black-shouldered falcon	58
milky way dreaming	59

Walking Larapinta Trail

we are but travellers here	63
Ormiston Pound	64
coolamon dreaming	66
daybreak over Mt Sondar	68
Palm Valley	69

Journey to Kati Thanda – Lake Eyre

Parachilna rumble	73
abandoned	75
vicissitudes of Lake Eyre	76
anomaly	77

Memorial

a villanelle for Oodgeroo Noonuccal	81
Haiku	82
Myall Creek A Suite	83
ghost of terra nullius	88
songlines	91
to Rachel Carson	92

Acknowledgements	94

There is a desert I long to be walking,
a wide emptiness:
Peace beyond any understanding of it.

Rumi

Introduction

Australians are becoming more coastal dwellers. We sit on this veranda, enjoy the coastal breeze. To venture too far into wilderness is a challenge. Even in the city, it is easy to become impatient with nature, for it follows its own laws. Trees drop leaves and branches, their roots wreck paths. Animals eat our plants (my ringtail possums love my parsley), cockatoos eat solar wires, brush turkeys renovate gardens. As for the bandicoots and echidnas that lived in our garden, they have left long ago. Even the blue-tongue lizards are rare now.

Thomas Berry, environmentalist and eco-theologian, writes, 'this generation has lost interaction with nature, we are talking to ourselves'.

We need to talk to the rivers, deserts, mountains, forests and grasslands. Walk in their way, listen to what they have to say, begin a new conversation and become intimate again with the natural world.

Such experiences bring us closer
to the heart of our land,
to the spirit of country,
to the soul of what it means to be a human being.

When we listen, this land sings to us, holds us, nurtures us. This land is the common ground that we share. This small blue planet is the common world of our existence.

Desert Patterns is a collection of poetry that touches the membrane between two worlds with the breath of wildness and our inland journeys.

Colleen Keating

Dadirri

Aboriginal writer and elder Miriam-Rose Ungunmerr-Baumann has given us the word *dadirri* – from the language of the Aboriginal people of the Daly River region, Darwin, NT.

Dadirri is inner, deep listening and quiet, still awareness. It recognises the deep spring that is inside us. We call on it and it calls to us.

Miriam-Rose explains, 'When I experience *dadirri*, I am made whole again. I can sit on the riverbank or walk through a stand of trees; even if someone close to me has passed away, I can find my peace in this silent awareness. There is no need of words. A big part of *dadirri* is listening.'

She continues, 'This was the normal way for us to learn – not by asking questions. We learnt by watching and listening, waiting and then acting. My people are not threatened by silence. They are completely at home in it. They have lived for thousands of years with Nature's quietness.'

Dadirri also means awareness of where you've come from, why you are here, where you are going and where you belong.

'Our Aboriginal culture has taught us to be still and to wait. We do not try to hurry things up. We let them follow their natural course – like the seasons.'

From Edge of the Sacred Conference at White Gums Honeymoon Gap, West MacDonnell Ranges, Alice Springs, 2016.

The Top End of Australia

My land is mine only because I came in spirit from the land
and so did my ancestors of the same land…
My land is my backbone…the reason I stand straight…

Galarrwuy Yunupingu

in the beginning

is it destiny that brings us here
from far-flung destinations
helping each other with stretchers and tents
each night laughing and chatting
no longer strangers after day one

or is it chance that beckons
brings us together
to prepare a kitchen for cooking each night
sitting over our meal with a glass of wine
being Abrahams marvelling at our desert sky

maybe it is words like Kimberley
Bungle Bungles Kakadu Tanami
that touch some romantic string
play in our hearts
conjure the earthy red of our souls

crew

in a way
it was the crew that made it happen

on our way out of Darwin
our driver exclaimed

well thrill seekers let's get on our way
we are in for a journey of a lifetime
through the Northern Territory
to a glimpse of Arnhem Land
across the Top End of Western Australia
through the Kimberleys to Broome
and down to the remote Tanami Desert
into the heart   the red heart
that deeply beats around Uluru

be astonished
be amazed
be bedazzled
my friends
by the mystery of history
the landscape
and infinity of time

and we were

blank page

kaleidoscope colours spin
a thousand rainbows pierce my mind
their sounds a harmony
unpredictable
in pattern and wildness

a poem in my head
it whispers   sometimes
cries   sometimes shouts

i chase my fancy
like a blue butterfly in flight
only to have to trade
the living beauty of imagination
for the disappointment
of the blank page

my three-dimensional images
colour   sound   movement
flatline
a dusty pinned butterfly
stretched on the wall

to find the words   to ruffle the page
is my challenge

a grand sweep of landscape

being in the Kimberley
is familiar and unfamiliar
like holding hands with someone
to feel their story

the fortune teller in me
wants to read every line
to glean the whole
trace my finger
the life line   the heart line
allow the present
to connect past
and future

being in the Kimberley
is familiar and unfamiliar
touching   listening   sharing
and the sacredness
of entering holy ground

this is not alien land

the muse beckons
from the north
sun   colour   texture
wings in
psyche   silence   word

it plays my imagination
with night skies   wild rivers
red soil   Indigenous history
and its landscapes

the muse beckons
from the north
taste   sound   story
wings in
sense   silence   word

from first peoples i learn
this is not alien land
we are the aliens
and but travellers here

Kakadu

first morning breaks
an eager tropical sky
sings inspiration
nudges the horizon

stretches imagination
high into ancient stone hills
its music in the dreaming

with first light
comes a boisterous wet season billabong
a dawn chorus
Peter Sculthorpe once listened
captured it in music
to welcome
dawn of the new millennium

i breathe the air
feel the sky's calm

there for the pondering
thousands of blazing-blue lilies
daub the lagoon
lily pads pave the surface so thickly
one could use them
as stepping stones

imagine if Claude Monet
was passing this way
in this light
he'd fall to his knees with joy

the Jesus bird

meeting the Jesus bird
walking on water
and watching it dance
around blue lotus blooms
where the Buddha is said to sit
and Brahmans reign
makes you tilt your head back
and laugh at the sky

it is the comb-crested jacana
its elegant limbs and splayed feet
dance on water with the lint of insects

a solitary white-bellied sea eagle hovers
tiny azure kingfishers scan
in majesty   ibis and brolgas
stalk the reeds

as smoke from burn-offs tinges the air
the sinking red sun
silhouettes pandanus
against an orange sky

magpie geese
with glossy iridescent wings
take to the air
their v-shaped wave
and high-pitched whistle
momentarily   crowds the sky

parallel realms

just before dusk   bounce of light
still playful   our tents already settled
the lily-studded lagoon begins to dim

if i had been at home in the city
i'd be writing about the billions spent
on the chill of submarines
imagine someone's grandchild drowning in them
who now struggles to learn in the heat
of a demountable classroom

if i had been in Sydney
i'd be writing against inhumanity
denying words like *irregular maritime arrivals*

here is theatre of another kind
curtain rises
for an operatic show   wading black-necked jabirus
forage
throw their heads back in delight

spindly coral-red legs
choreographed to water music
dance   lift off
hover on fan-like wings   linger
on the air's wedge
become silhouettes of the sun
as silence surges in

this realm is enough for me
sometimes i wish there were no gateway back
then again i am not needed here

cicada dreaming

today we enter a three-tiered land
Katherine Gorge
core for eons of the Jawoyn* people
who know its backboned cliffs
that rise to full height
fired red on inky water
who know its heart and soul
and reclaim its ancient name
Nitmiluk *place of the cicada dreaming*

why does it so stir me?
even the air is intangible
is it a place the gods keep
to seduce the lost like me?
is it a portal to another realm
like places of thin membrane
in old world stories?

vegetation   dull and dusty
calico scrub painted
on red rocky land
and majestic mountains
their cool secret gorges
and lush rainforests
shadowed with mystery

* also known as Djauan people

Nitmiluk

1 falling

waking was falling
not into limbo or from a dream
falling in space
down marbleised rock without grip
the picturesque Katherine Gorge
seen upside down
acrobatic
not pretty when bones break

getting up was going down
the crunch was unforgiving
jarring   ominous
just a sprain I said
I knew differently
the relieved group to the rescue
ice and the young handsome Tim
the cruise captain
searching out every possibility
from his first aid kit and a sling
that helps me to enjoy the cruise

2 learning to fly

the boat stops
drifts towards the bank
lulled by lapping against the side
we gaze
into the ooze of mud to watch crocodiles
slyly watch us

we drift closer
for photographers to capture
yellow glint of eye
and brown steel rivets of spine tailing mud

with the stillness on the lake
our eyes catch the sway
of a high-up branch from the bank

two brolgas   all the elegance
of flamingo dancers
their red heads flashing
push their fledgling chicks from the nest
perched high in the branches of a kurrawong

there was no falling
air currents carried them
to the next branch

at every attempt
to return to their security
a brolga parent opened wide white wings
fanning them off
as chicks squawked and flailed
again and again

amidst the spectacle of protest
i ponder my dream to fly rather then fall
to feel the lightness of being
throw this body off like a skin
rather then end up in Kununurra Hospital
having X-rays and advice
from Perth orthopaedic surgeons
on how to proceed with a broken wrist

Kununurra

towns are dying   even mining towns
with the curse of fly-ins
towns are putting their hands
up for rescue

not Kununurra

this place of parched pindan* earth
is irrigated by the Ord River Dam and Lake Argyle
Perth's winter vegie gardens keep it alive
Sandalwood plantations thrive

towns are dying   not Kununurra
this town is thriving
and the hospital to set my broken wrist
was world-class standard

* red sandy country characteristic of southwest Kimberley area, maybe from an Aboriginal term– *bardi/ bindan* – for the bush

Yellow Water Billabong

in the Yellow Water Billabong
the cruise boat glides smoothly

the putter of the engine shuts off
chatter settles
only breath hums   a Sculthorpe calm
that jabs the big blue Capricornia sky alive
of this Kakadu National Park

a breeze scrolls the water
rhythmic lap lap against the boat
a heart beat of country

we drift closer to the bank
silently watch crocodiles
ooze through the mud

splash of a cormorant dive
fluff of young magpie geese
run bravely nearby
an egret stalks for prey
and flocks of ducks have no fear
amongst the mangroves
while crocodiles
laze slyly as muddy snouts
with not even a ripple

here is wilderness   freedom
an ancient and primal land

Gibb River Road

it throws you and your four-wheel
mercilessly   like a wild ocean
tosses a small craft

you bump down into each trough
deal with its rough battering
and accelerate
to crest it with relief
doused in dust

climbing out of the Pentecost River
towards Coburn Range
you crest violently   bus covered in mud

even as you are reassured
a grader has been through
to tame this tempestuous landscape
ripped to its bone by annual monsoons

here the red sand tracks
are notorious to grab wheels
like quick sand
and bring you to a full stop

at the crossings you are warned
not to wade in to check depth
or you will end up   *croc dinner*

Litchfield National Park 1

tread lightly

whistling kites
firebirds of the sky

hang
on updrafts of air

eyeing prey
in blackened patchwork of burn-off

we wander
through hundreds of termite mounds
their north-south stance
a graveyard of magnetic headstones

tread lightly
this land a remnant of Gondwanaland*
is a library of books still to be written

---

* Gondwanaland is the name given to an ancient supercontinent.

Litchfield National Park 2

waterfall

monsoons thunder down all summer
cyclones whirl in from the sea   drop
destructive angry loads
curl back out with a whimper

we stand and marvel
at geological wonders   created
sandstone blocks of the lost city
the hiss and steam of waterfall

water tiers plummet
deafen our ears
our words are swallowed
we are swallowed
in wonder at this gulp of thunder

here are one hundred and thirty-five steps
to swim
some led down as if by prayer
to plunge into its gaping mouth
where downwater torrentially falls
Florence Falls is the answer for the brave
no swimming at the inviting Wangi Falls
crocs have been seen swimming here

seeking permission

the journey
from our camp to the sacred site
with galleries of rock paintings
the local Wunambal people call Munurru*
takes us through dense swamp grass
all around virgin-white egrets lift off
trailing clouds of glory
their wide wings
whisper our coming

at the entrance to the caves
i pick up red earth
let it slowly sift through my fingers
murmur my name
ask permission to enter
the breath of welcome is all around
as if the earth remembers me
holds me tenderly

red dirt absorbs our footfall
a hush of reverence falls over the group

* Munurru west of Kalumburu Road and Mitchell Plateau Road, Kimberley region, WA – name given by the local Wunambal people. Here are many examples of north Kimberley rock art. A book called *Aboriginal Paintings at Mururru* by David M. Welsh is available at local roadhouses.

mystery of Munurru

golden-sunrise grass welcomes us
and grey Buddha termite mounds
amidst scrawny ragged woodlands
of grey box   white gum and paperbarks
with surprise of flowers
yellow red and orange
food for bird   possum and bat fly-ins

and after a trek in by foot
we meet hidden quartzite boulders
mystical in their cluster
as if carried in and placed by the gods
they say from an aerial view
it could be an ancient Stonehenge

we have come to Munurru
the sacred hem of a rock art gallery
more than fifty thousand years old
rock art of brolgas   echidnas   painted hands
muted ochres of red yellow black white
and Wandjina*

the air vibrates
with ancestors of the Dreaming

questions crowd in
mystery the only answer

* creative spirits of cloud and rain, symbols of fertility depicted in Kimberley rock art

touch this earth

obviously none of us have any idea
he says   on the way back to the bus
as if avoiding further conversation
(about words like dreamtime)
just call it an art gallery from before time

the track weaves back through spindly scrub
crumbly quartzite under foot
a vastness stretches
as if it could go on forever
without breaking silence

what can we do to restore respect
for our oldest civilisation
and this country once noted unstoried
artless   unfarmed   enhanced*

it holds its secret
like the red salmon gums
their smooth waxy bark
determined not to split or peel
not to give themselves away

like the banyan tree firmly planting
itself over and over
with its shaggy feet into terra firma

and the sustainer   pandanus
that spirals its fibonacci twist
giving seed   string   fruit
fibre for weaving

like cycads the stand-out remnant
of the long fossil history book

take off your shoes
let your feet touch this earth
feel the stab and stick and stone of story
and wake for pity's sake
wake
be stirred by this earth
awake to its mystery awake to its miracle
wake for pity's sake**

* *The Dark Emu* by Bruce Pascoe rights this inaccuracy and false impression that still lingers in some parts of Australian history.
** *The Sleep of Prisoners*: Christopher Fry

Geikie Gorge

maybe it's the way the light falls
throws its arms around the old familiar cliffs
brings them alive   beckons come
come

even as we cruise along
its colour shifts through the spectrum
like time through a history book
a 350-million-year history book
its pages patinaed in Devonian decor
each page a story in texture and colour
a pop up three-dimensional storybook

our curator   the Indigenous guide
points out the pivots of time

and mirrored in the Fitzroy river
our group   could be white-gloved
archivists   with awed whispers
humble at the mystery before them

Mabel Downs Station

no power in this wilderness
imagine no facebook   no wifi
not even email
only stars
brilliant stars
piercing a navy velvet sky

quiet stillness settles into our very soul
kangaroos thrum the darkness
that wreaths our fire hearth
and laughter of the group

and me finished for the day
not wanting to talk any more
just be quiet
cocooned in the dark of the cosmos
with its milky silk scarf
and pinpointer stars that journey us

brahmins   buddhas   boabs

only clouds of shrieking corellas
burst from scrawny eucalypts
and grasslands
as we tourists   wannabe pilgrims
drive through
intensely coloured ranges
dramatic gorges   with orange-
red the dominant colours

brahmin with podgy jowls munch
on golden sunrise grass
hardly glance our way
splodgy brown termite mounds
like fat laughing buddhas
and boab trees with stodgy presence
exude a sense of repose

all centre an unharried spirit of place
as life for us seems to rush by

Purnululu National Park

transported culturally and spiritually
that's what happens
when you jolt along on a dirt track
into a grand sweep of landscape they call
the Purnululu* and Bungle Bungles
the heart of the Kimberley
sculptures of the Dreamtime

a range of burnt umber mountains
wind and water-fretted rocks
with buzz of beehive stripes
ochre   sienna   and turmeric
striated with charcoal pigment

soft curves and towering domes
toned down by ambered honey

our group trek into ancient realms
into gorges and chasms
cool secrets of cathedral grandness
humbly realising we are
a fret of sand in a sandy desert
a nano in geological time

* comes from Gija people, meaning fretting sands

Bungle Bungles

the great stone formation knows where it stands
and what's more   it knows what it is

it belongs   time holds
its story   like it holds the light
in precious stone

the Bungle Bungles fits itself to the earth
a string of tiger-eyed jewels placed
into the nape of a lady's bare neck
an adornment on its landscape

it rests
like a gathering of umbered ducks
tranquil on water
yet paddling wildly

we hike for a kilometre in its underworld
find in scalloped black-winged corners
sleeping bats in their thousands

find in Echidna Chasm
that when we sit quietly   the tingle
of glow worms lights up its Milky Way

in lofty coolness of Cathedral Gorge
we stand   like the time we stood in Rome
beneath the dome in the Pantheon
marvelling over and over

yet here we are reminded
the Bungle Bungles   make
domes and cathedrals of history even
those standing stones
of ancient times
look youthful
for here is beyond history
here belongs the sweep of Dreamtime

Jandamarra 1

Tunnel Creek

Windjana Gorge   fresh   pristine
permanent water   percolated
from ancient rains that deluged the land

slippery marbleised boulders
bluff the uninitiated
sustain mystery
deter and challenge efforts to go further
into the secret of Tunnel Creek

without hand or foot grip
trust plumbs the abyss
tumbles into coolness

a sombre space
deeply carved from Devonian times
salted with yellow light
its rays tinkling like tiny bells
decor of stalactites and stalagmites
pendants of bats and glint of eyes
timid fresh water crocs
in this sandy echoing amphitheatre
with long bare arm i scoop up spring water
and hear of Jandamarra

his spirit is here
this was his last place to stand

Jandamarra 2

Flashback

Tunnel Creek
the Kimberley outback
land of the Bunuba people
the time is late nineteenth century
the last stage of white invasion
being played out
herds of cattle trample the grasses
waterholes gone

spirit is broken
faded sepia shots capture   for history
naked black men   neck and ankle chained
on a track to Derby lock-up
powerless

yet one warrior
Jandamarra takes a last stand
turns against his white masters
fights heroically
to save his people
and his country

a mythical figure   he appeared   fought
disappeared   unable to be tracked
for years he held out
the one burning flame

betrayal and a bullet
a fight that died to a flicker
it was in his Tunnel Creek cave
Jini his mother held him as life petered out
a Pietà on the rock of Golgotha

Jandamarra 3

Bunuba Country

a city poet can not glean
the essence of the Bunuba people
their story is easily lost
in white history and chronological time

the plunge into Tunnel Creek
further connects to mystery
it is about feeling
rather then hearing stories told

and still today
documented as criminals
who died because they defied
legitimate laws and white society
redacts another history

closed full stop

are you really disappearing   are you a torn-up town
has there been a drink from the *shrink me* bottle

gold drew in the dreamer   iron ore drilled into your soul
meat works rescued for a time
exports a link to the hungry north
Wyndham   are you just another dying town

barricaded empty houses   empty shops
wire fences   rusted padlocks
closed   says the tin shed café and lee's tonic shop
tools   petrol bowsers   machinery   all abandoned
rusting cars   boarded up pubs
and graffitied on one window   *closed full stop*

red ochre   fat boabs   bougainvillea
frangipani   wild and cyclone-whipped
this country is loud in its cry   stomped down by change

gazing from your lookout at the Cambridge Gulf
i wanted a beautiful site
five rivers with mouths whispering   five languages of love
feeding the Timor Sea

your harbour on the edge so much abandoned
rust-swallowed terminals   factories   rail tracks
three ships   now corroded hulks
stand witness

cathedrals pyramids and buddhas

they sound international
with distinctive shape   texture   detail
these termite mounds of the top end

we love to hear the stories
how they are magnetic in direction
engineered structures
house millions of workers
industrious as any great city

how architecturally designed
to regulate flow of water
for wet season and dry
a balance to trap   cool and circulate air
even store their winter food
a low carbon footprint for sure

we learn the workers use clay
chewed plants   poo and sticky saliva
for their cement
permanent against the elements
and any hungry predators that lurk
while an army of termite soldiers
who smell a problem
defend with squirts of chemical
and clamour in their thousands
to the breach to mend walls

on the landscape they stand
in their hundreds
demand you come and marvel
like tourists do internationally
at red cathedrals
cinnamon-brown pyramids
and bulbous laughing buddhas

from the bus

a coolabah tree takes off into the desert air
as hundreds of white corellas
like screeching branches
tack into the sun

whistling kites swoop
we drive into their wake
of fire-dappled light
in a lilac sky
red clouds trail
thin as tulle

two brolgas
stand by the road
elegant statues
in Devonian country

earth song
song of creation
for me an act of love

Broome

the sun
into the sea
drowns

fiery throes
heartbeats
pulsate
as blood spurts
along veins of our land

its aura
lingers
as with hundreds of others
we pop champagne
and watch

ponderings

in Broome   history of the dive trade
sea-pearl jewellery
now an anathema to me

Fitzroy Crossing
on horizon of a moonless sky
sharp claws of scorpio

spiny-leaved spinifex
key to survival
termites munch

mulga dreaming

again we make camp
hard rocky ground of mulga country
the Tanami Desert

a wedge-tail struts around roadkill
a murder of crows gather for their share
hot vapour sizzles
air blurs into zigzags
speaking of life   here it is sacrificial

here death and life copulate
the world is given back to itself
silence deceives those who fear death

put your ear to the scorched earth
listen   to the gnaw and munch
termites devour spinifex
that spike air above ground
mounds camouflage versatility
shades ants   geckos salivate   lizards wait
birds of prey hover
speaking of life   here it is communal

desert patterns

the landscape dreams
of caterpillars and rainbow serpents
composed
sculptured
moulded for aeons
wind water sand
carved chiselled hefted
hewn
from rock and clay
heave of ochre red
weave curve wave

desert patterns
draw us in

every escarpment every contour
named and known
as a mother knows its children
garments of beauty
that dress our earth
like whims of scarves

desert patterns
draw us in

the night sky dreams
of journeys emus echidnas
black spaces
compose
shimmer
imagination
reflects ancient stories

desert patterns
draw us in

bush tucker

in this land of bloodwood   pandanus   boab
wooded grasslands   under blue diamond skies
laced in colours of indian spice
there is the coloniser and the colonised
there is struggle between two ways
to do or to be
one who knows by blade one by blood

to 'do' the land for every secret it might hide
to work   mine   dam   tame   change it
for money with a nexus
of overstocking   greed
easily becomes   enemy of the earth

today it is the latter
the modern stewards of the land
informed by life
thousands of years of life   harvest
grass seed and native plants   share
ways of cultivation   grass burnings
ash compost   water ponding

as fire kite birds soar the smoky updrafts
our local guide suggests his supplies
are an early version of Bunnings and Coles
we taste seeds   berries   fruits   floury boab nut
learn of lotus and honey and protein source
hidden in bark of trees and in the ground
plant medicines   tools   shaped bowls
there is pride in grasses
flowing golden waves   knee-deep

once described
land of the never never   arid desert
dead heart   wasted inland   back of beyond

the Kimberleys keeps us guessing
at its vibrance   its life
its story into the far reaches of the Dreaming

desert domes

the turn off sign on the Great North Highway
flags us down for a photo shoot
Tanami Track one thousand and thirty-two kilometres

Alice Springs   three days away
it is said   this is an ancient songline
always Kukatja and Walpiri country
known as mother from the dreaming

put your ear to her red heart
hear the termites munching,
on them there spiky spinifex
they begin our food chain
their tough stalagmite mounds
industrious as New York City

as we journey   distant trees change partners
on a glinting mirage dance floor

a big sky contains us
dusting us in red dirt
in our shook up dome

a 360- degree choice of direction
to a human nowhere
rewards us with a fiery setting sun
and at night
a dome of star dust

at Rabbits Flat

black silhouetted branches
haunt the horizon

termite mounds are different here
hundreds of tall red pointed sentinels
tower over a flat   flat landscape

listen
how deep the silence
dense as the black-holed sky

if you listen beyond
the crunch-munch of a secret world
can be heard

the mulga trees
like upside-down umbrellas
hold out for erratic dew drops
to funnel down
and their gunmetal leaves
curl away like shy maidens

here is a big sky shot with silver
and streamed with shooting stars
a threshold for a mind
to sit   wonder at the count of stars

draw your finger   a circle of horizon
here it is easy to imagine
you are centre of the world

Uluru

nurturing heart
haloed
by the milky way

In your presence a hush falls: a deep sigh of one struck by awe. My eyes trace your swelling curve. Womb of the earth, patient and poised, pregnant with possibility, constant in changing light.

A new silence settles, we hear your heart beat. Before, we did not listen. We saw only a massive landmark, a challenge to conquer. Two hundred and twenty years on, we listen to our first peoples who speak from the country where wind moans through the spiky spinifex and kestrels soar on the updrafts. There is awareness of the earth as mother, her breath heaving in cyclic moods, birthing our being as a renewed nation. We remember. Unchaining frees us to go forward. Truth heals the scars. Listen. Weeping turns to song, sadness to dance.

symphony of frogs
your barometer
sing in renewal

* haibun – Japanese form of writing

the black-shouldered falcon

with dawn
an air-faring peregrine
comes into my view
upwind riding
on wing of hot desert air

wingspan in full command
on lightness of air
with tail fluting ripples of gold
a frisson of dawn-light
shimmers

it hangs on waves of air
like a sky-rider

hovers
in search of prey
soars higher and higher
for its arrow dive

milky way dreaming

sun ablaze
dark skin
shines with sweat
her eyes look up   catch me

she sits on the earth
a red sandy space
at the edge of the Alice Springs Mall
her canvas held down
by four small rocks

milky way dreaming

a sash of silver gossamer
arches across the black canvas
in a brilliance of stars
to the side   seven dotted circles
she points
names the seven sisters

only desert eyes know this sky
paint this song of stars
didgeridoo dancing stars
brimming
fiery-white and deep

now on my wall
framed

Walking Larapinta Trail

Our story is told through rock art painted on granite parchment.
Our story is written in the land.
We have sacred and special places.
Look after story, look after Country,
it will look after you, that's how we survived for over 70,000 years.

Bob Faulkner, Anaiwan and Kamilaroi elder

we are but travellers here

in desert country
outside Alice Springs
richly red rock   rusted fiery
bruised and brushworked to indigo
shimmers through hot air

a track like an ancient songline
marks a way
frisks intruders

needle spinifex claw
roots of river gums
bulbous siphons plunge defiantly
deep into dry river beds

we trudge heavily
sand shifts unevenly

bones picked clean
washed up   caught against tree trunks
from the last big wet
a warning this land is merciless
nemesis
teacher

at the end of each day
a truck delivers swags
food   water
reminding us we are but travellers here*

* we are but travellers here – Mary McKillop

Ormiston Pound

we climb an ancient path
to the rattle of our tin mugs
dangling from our backpacks
and the crinkle of boots disturbing stones
as they shift awkwardly underfoot

quartzite
flanks each side
summons up rough sharp spurs

serrated edges
like bread knives
cut the sky
give direction

flints of mica catch the light
blinding and brooding black rocks watch
as menacing phantoms

at the top
we sit breathless
and hot
the wide expanse of Ormiston Pound
like an enormous bunker
lies below
air drifts with heat and layers of cool
we sit and listen to white man's story

while an acacia bush nearby
growing from a rock outcrop
sings to me another story
on Dreamtime wind

there is a private language here
an endless delicate exchange
that I do not understand

coolamon dreaming

desert night
over our Finke River camp in Ormiston Pound
dwarfed by imposing walls of rock
a thousand succulent stars drip

heat cools   sighs
as gentle on our cheeks
as a lover's breath on a balmy night

our faces flicker in the low ember fire

smug in geological knowledge
that we are camped in a meteor crater
we lounge back wrapped in a mantle of stars
and listen
the elder
weaves her Dreamtime stories
into the tapestry of creation

her eyes   hypnotic   dark as the night
draw us in

the baby star fell
our ancestors tell of a fierce light
its crash to this place

she points up
see the coolamon* from where it fell
her finger curves the outline
of a black space in the sky

and still each day
its parents   the morning and evening star
circle the earth in search
of their fallen child

i sleep the dreaming
breathe the ancient air
in awe   feel connected
aware of the stars as my ancestors

i wake
to hues of mustard and ochre red
last curdles of smoke from the ashen fire
and watch transfixed
the morning star
journey in dawn's cobalt-blue sky

* a basin-shaped wooden carry dish made and used by some first peoples (Macquarie)

daybreak over Mt Sondar

in the beginning
air static as a nylon petticoat pulled over my hair
fingerprints of ruby red
betray the world   dark-coloured
the arc of dawn flexes
stirs Mt Sondar
an awakening blush
flutters fire red   catching
Namatjira's* mountain
blood-red

as I sit here   it pulsates
the sun not yet over the horizon
like an intruder rushes in
steals every shade and shadow

this mountain lies in the country with poise
immortalised in a gown of purple and blue
like a sleeping goddess behind glass

yet the rattle of chains and padlock
thump like a heartbeat against my ribs
as in the nearby town
for a dollar
kids still buy a rusty jam tin of petrol

* Albert Namatjira was a famous Aboriginal artist from the MacDonnell Ranges in Central Australia. Mt Sondar features in many of his iconic paintings.

Palm Valley

are you up to it?
it's hot
forty degrees or more
the tour guide looks at the group

i so wanted this day to go ahead
and it did
in four-wheel drive
we roughed it
along the sandy Finke River Gorge
into Palm Valley
for our Mpulungkunya walk
into an oasis shaded
and fanned
by hundreds of slender
red cabbage palm   relics
of ancient cycads

carrying our water
we trekked through
hot dry air
under a relentless sun
shadows
of hot ochred rock
proud sculptures of the desert
our occasional respite

forty degrees and climbing   maybe
but here amidst amphitheatres
pinnacles and gorges
we enjoyed a rust-red oasis
lush in its verdancy

cooled our feet dangled in a baptism
of coming home to country our land

Journey to Kati Thanda – Lake Eyre

Parachilna rumble

dangerous to blink
driving into Parachilna*
population seven
not even the dusty brown dog
gets up to greet us

the furrowed road
edged with dusty tufts of salt bush
stretches to the horizon
in this boundless land

Parachilna is a welcome stop

a hot hazy town
a red earth town
it glows a red clay aura
burnished red and dusty
even the old pepper trees
are dusty

the Prairie Pub
is famous for its FMG
Feral Mixed Grill
an antipasto of camel emu goat and kangaroo
quandongs natural limes and bush tomatoes
yet the sparkle of chilled white wine
makes the stop worthwhile

the barmen like a town crier
calls
train on
and the pub quickly empties
to regroup
across the wide wide dusty street

a distant hum intrudes

chardonnay in hand
we watch the freight train
heavy with coal
ponderously lumber
like a gentle swarthy beast
towards us
the parachilna rumble begins
a heavy slow rumble
all three kilometres of it
with muffled grumbles and slow clanks
hypnotic music of the outback
like children we practise counting
this head to tail migration
all two hundred and twenty cars
it recedes in its own time
as the desert reclaims its silence

* Parachilna was once a town now a pub in South Australia between Port Augusta and Leigh Creek and west of the Flinders Ranges.

abandoned

a fallen water tank
rusted blood-red
rippled
as sere ribs of a dead beast
lies half buried
in the shifting ochre red earth
against stony ruins
dominantly built

a witness
to the firefly hope
and belief
abandoned

to conquer nature

(In South Australia there are many ruins, remains of those who built unaware of the Goyder line that would be declared in 1865.)

vicissitudes of Lake Eyre

bleached salt pans
glint in a hostile sun
their mirage
a phantom deathtrap
in a land of unreachable horizons

yet sometimes flood waters flow
crack the parched earth
eddy into the cavernous silence
and like touch arouses longing
water stirs
awakens a dormant world
into golumptuous life

fish like transparent slivers of glass
brine shrimp   trilling tadpoles
become a teaming ocean
luring flocks of birds to roost and feed

a million water birds in a desert sky
a paradise
till drought
Kali* with a flaming sword
banishes life once again

Lake Eyre has celebrated the revival of its ancient Aboriginal name, Kati Thanda. Lake Eyre – which when full becomes one of the largest inland seas in the world – is now recognised by its old name but its official name will be Kati Thanda-Lake Eyre.

* Kali, Hindu goddess of destruction and creation

anomaly

how did this pelican
find its way here

as it lifted from the distant Coorong
could it smell or taste
the far away northern rains
did it know that this banquet
would be its ultimate journey

it yawns
as if it's just another day

with fragile pride
it hunches on a rock
alert
playing the run of water
thundering into the once dry salt pan
looking quite at home

Memorial

If a child is to keep alive his/her inborn sense of wonder, he/she needs the companionship of at least one adult who can share the joy, excitement, and mystery of the world we live in.

Rachel Carson, author of *The Silent Spring*

a villanelle for Oodgeroo Noonuccal

your eyes look out at me through time
from gallery wall   with gaze intent
eyes sad yet alert with hope hold mine

black history is told as if we're blind
from ash of heartbreak you saw ascent
your eyes look out at me through time

campfire yarns tell of brave and fine
your poetic words say what is meant
eyes sad yet alert with hope hold mine

your noble struggle from deeds malign
your call to belong an open stent
your eyes look out at me through time

when hand in hand our paths entwine
troubles you knew can then be spent
eyes sad yet alert with hope hold mine

can blood on wattle of humankind
be washed with words of new intent
your eyes look out at me through time
eyes sad yet alert with hope hold mine

Under the name Kath Walker, Oodgeroo Noonuccal (1920–1993),
poet and activist, was the first Aboriginal Australian to publish a
book of verse. Her poem 'Son of Mine' inspired this villanelle.

Haiku

Myall Creek –
our windscreen vision
veiled in frost

Myall Creek   A Suite

1.
after the massacre

when we wake to truths
that make our hearts beat fast
walk the blood-red gravel track
that draws us down
to write the story on our heart
needled on our skin
to pin our bones into its frame

and stand
with Milton's fear
for blindness and denial
then grope and touch
the blood-stained earth
with spines of ironbark
and smell the stench of burnt flesh
where only eucalypts should waft

we weep

then truth that quickens
our nation's gut
stirs the country's womb
in all its wrench of birthing pangs
rips and tears at every sinew

all we know
there is no going back

2.
in search of history   July 2017

'did we not know their blood channelled our rivers' – Judith Wright

how do you remember
days that history clouded
smothered in bleached blankets
and bundled into recesses
dark alcove corners of our nation's history
and dared anyone to lurk there?

how can you remember
trojan horses   stand all over our country
with their story inside
that bursts to be told
side by side
with every town's war memorial

we go in search of one of those stories

you don't find this place by accident
it's a journey from the coast
drive inland, west as we say
step off your veranda
away from safety and comfort of home.

Myall Creek Reserve
a picnic area to enjoy lunch
and cuppa from our new thermos
amid stringy barks   eucalypts
and grass trees
no corner shop for many a mile.

a peacefulness halos us
in the distance sheep graze
in a patch of irrigated green
cattle munch

yet here is the place of a massacre
finally acknowledged   named   dated
clutched out of the recesses of memory
and into history

3.
shared history   June 2018
(Read at Myall Creek memorial)

History despite its wrenching pain
cannot be unlived,
but if faced with courage,
need not be lived again – Maya Angelou

there's something in the shining light
that lends itself to thoughts of hope
perhaps it is a brashness – the way it glows
so cheerfully in this cloudless winter time
perhaps the way it dresses up the land
catches blue kingfishers on their wing
festoons the leaves   the rocks   the trees

today it lights the darkest claw of time
burns away clouds of brutal wrong
touches blood-stained earth
of blame   of shame
too long consumed
too many years   too many tears

one hundred and eighty years on
we walk the Myall Creek Memorial Way
the light plays the red gravel of its track
and flickers on tiny wrens in nearby scrub

there's a quietness amidst our camaraderie
swish of ropes   yells   grapple of chains
are stilled now
murdering rage and gall are quieted
smell of gun powder spent
yet screams that cried that stark cold night
still sigh amidst the sway
of stringy bark and eucalypt

there's something in the shining light
that lends itself to thoughts of hope
perhaps it is the cleansing smoke   the way
we catch the mica glint on granite stone
and how we stop and read and bow our heads
no longer in the blinding dark and listen
to a people's heart and our shared history

ghost of terra nullius

(in the search for a nuclear waste dump)

i arrived at Newtown community centre
free coffee   plenty of flyers   lots of chatter
took my seat as a welcomed outsider

beckoned by an email   that plucked the right chord
amidst all the other vibrations including
fracking   farm lands   our rivers   silting our reef
and fight against waste

a woman from Muckaty country stood
quoted a prominent politician

why on earth can't people in the middle of nowhere
accept low and intermediate level waste

and then she faced us
answered his question

this is not *nowhere* mister politician
on your Canberra map it might look remote
and empty
out of sight out of mind
this is not uninhabited space

this is *somewhere*   a sacred somewhere
we are here in this back of beyond
our ancestors breathe and live in the red dust
we are the land   our dreaming
our journey   our story
this land is our song
the journal we write
the pictures we paint
this red earth is home to our people
creator and   creation
no separation for us

do not come here mister politician
treading this desert
puts red soil on the soles of your shoes
and you wouldn't want that

red dust gets into your soul
makes you feel somewhere
it might choke you when the wind blows

here our horizon is circular   shimmers its mirage
our population is sparse

yes it gives you space
for your uranium dump   I hear you say
but we have reason to revolt at ignorance
we hear of Montebello Island   Emu Field   Maralinga
maybe just words to you

our song is our blood poured forth
our hearts pound for our children
for us life is timeless
for you I sense a rage of time

but we have our animals and our food
we have our water   our soil
our precious billabongs and springs
they are not for your contamination

songlines

trace the spirit of land
follow rivers
landscapes
types of soil
cool springs
star maps

our work is to recover this song navigation
the seasonal changes
the early farming ways
care of country
reconnect ourselves

the earth is our mother
mother of all
says Hildegard of Bingen
the twelfth century German mystic
across the cultures
she cradles   holds   succours us

settle   listen to the space between your breaths
hear the whisper of earth
tread lightly for we walk sacred ground

to Rachel Carson

sometimes the magpies bring you
and the earth cries
always cries
with a mother's groan
of pain

the earth cries
she the feminine
vulnerable
abused
victim
our mother
the one that nourishes
hunger from dark soils
the one that quenches
thirst from the sky
holds us wrapped in her cycles

sometimes the magpies bring you
and the earth cries
cries
with a mother's groan
of pain

i remember
my enthusiasm for your voice
your cry in the *Silent Spring**
at last someone
you Rachel
articulates it

we both recollect
our faraway childhood days
heads of golden wheat nodding
our rivers flowing
we are all in this
together

this is a time to teach our children wonder
this is a time for awe
for confidence
reverence for all creatures
our land   our waters   soil and air

in hope
our cry is loud and is heard

* *Silent Spring* is an environmental science book by Rachel Carson. The book was published on 27 September 1962, documenting the adverse environmental effects caused by the indiscriminate use of pesticides. Carson accused the chemical industry of spreading disinformation, and public officials of accepting the industry's marketing claims unquestioningly. For many of us, it was her voice that made us aware and spurred us on towards movements for conservation and the environment in the late 60s.

Acknowledgements

Many of the poems in *Desert Patterns* have been enjoyed individually in publications: *Eureka Street*, *The Mozzie*, *Poetry Matters*, *The Good Oil* (SGS), *FreeXpresSion*, *Windfall*, *Eucalypt* and recently *Echidna Tracks*. I am grateful to the editors for their encouragement and dedication to poetry.

It is lovely to have them together as story. Our camping venture in the Far North, our experience with Lake Eyre in flood, my walking the Larapinta Track for ten days with writer and poet Jan Cornell woven in with story from our Indigenous guides.

The poem 'Sunrise over Mt Sonder' is award-winning. The poem 'shared history' was written for and read at the 180th Myall Creek Gathering and Memorial, 2018. It was also chosen for the Myall Creek website.

I would like to thank Norm Neill and fellow poets of the Wednesday evening poetry group, Sue Good, Decima Wraxall and the Women Writers Network, Pip Griffin and City FAW, the support of U3A Eastwood Poetry Appreciation Group and affirmation of Jan Conway, President of the Society of Women Writers.

My loving appreciation to Michael for his constant presence and inspiration.

www.ingramcontent.com/pod-product-compliance
Lightning Source LLC
Chambersburg PA
CBHW070942080526
44589CB00013B/1616